Buddha In Blue Jeans

An Extremely Short Simple Zen Guide to Sitting Quietly and Being Buddha

ISBN-13:978-1466480032
ISBN-10:1466480033

Website: www.taisheridan.com

Email: tai@taisheridan.com

DEDICATION

To the Great Silence

Listen to the sound of silence

- Paul Simon

Contents

INTRODUCTION

This is an extremely short, simple, and straight forward book.

It is a universal guide to the practice of sitting quietly and being yourself, which is the same as being Buddha. Sitting quietly can teach you many ways to accept life, meet pain, age gracefully, and die without regret.

I wrote this book for one reason: to encourage you to sit quietly every day.

Please enjoy being Buddha in Blue Jeans: a person of presence, openness, love, and benefit.

Tai Sheridan
Kentfield, California 2011

Sit Quietly

This is the most important Zen practice.

It is the classroom for living
a wise and kind life.

Sit anywhere and be quiet:
on a couch, a bed, a bench, inside, outside, leaning against
a tree, by a lake, at the ocean, in a garden, on an airplane,
in your office chair, on the floor, in your car.
Meditation cushions are okay too.

Sit at any time: morning, night,
one minute, three years.

Wear what you've got on.
Loosen your waist so that
your belly can move with your breath.

Sit as relaxed as possible.
Relax your muscles when
starting and during sitting.

Sit with your back straight but not stiff.
Keep your head upright with your ears level.

Respect all medical conditions.
Only take a posture you can.
All postures are okay.

Do what you can do.

Keep your eyes slightly opened and out of focus. Closing them will make you sleepy and sometimes busy. Opening them wide will keep you busy.

Breathe naturally through your nose.
Enjoy breathing.
Feel your breath.
Watch your breath.
Become your breath.

Be like a cat purring.
Follow your breath like ocean waves
coming in and out.

When you get distracted,
come back to the simplest
and most basic experience
of being alive,
your breathing.

That's it.
No belief.
No program.
No dogma.

You do not have to be Buddhist.
You can be of any faith, religion,
race, nationality, gender,
relationship status, or capacity.

Just sit quietly,
connect with your breath,
and pay attention
to what happens.

You will learn things.

Do it when you want.
You decide how much
is enough for you.

If you do it daily
it will get into your bones.

Please enjoy sitting quietly!

You will learn this sitting quietly.

CARE FOR YOUR BODY

Your body is your life.
Please take good care of it.

Inhabit your body.
Live gently inside of it.
Become best friends with it.

Hurt your body as little as possible.
You will be surprised
by the ways
in which you are
not connected to your body.
This is lifelong learning.

Sleep well and enough.
Eat well and not too much.
Move and stretch enough.

Accept and take care
of your medical difficulties.

You know what your body needs
to be healthy and alive.

Please enjoy taking care of your body!

You will learn this sitting quietly.

Accept Your Feelings

Your feelings are your heart and gut
response to the world.

Everything you feel is okay.
Feelings can be difficult.
Accept your feelings.

Sometimes you can trust them
as honest responses to people and events.
Sometimes you can't trust them,
they are reactions to people and events.
Keep sorting this out.

Your feelings will tell you
what you really need.
Learn to be gracious
with your unmet needs.

Kindly ask for what you want.
Respect everybody's right to say
yes or no to your needs.

Give up self centeredness
as much as possible.

Please enjoy your feelings!

You will learn this sitting quietly.

GIVE THOUGHTS ROOM

Your thoughts are just your thoughts.

They are not your life.
They are your thoughts.
Make a room as big
as the sky in your mind.
Your thoughts can be
clouds that float through.

Some of your thoughts are clear.
Some of your thoughts are muddy.
Belief is just thought.

An open mind isn't attached
to thinking or belief.

Thoughts can be a jail.
Watching them coming and going
lets you out to play in the universe.

Please enjoy watching
your thoughts come and go!

You will learn this sitting quietly.

PAIN IS NATURAL

Pain is a natural part of life.
Learn to accept it.
Learn to take care of it
as best you can.

Decrease the complaining.
Decrease the self-centeredness around it.
Everybody has pain.

Breathe and relax
into the pain
as best you can.

Please accept natural pain!

You will learn this sitting quietly.

BE WHO YOU ARE

Don't waste your life
trying to become somebody else.

Don't waste your life
trying to live up to
your performance expectations.

Don't waste your life
imitating others.

Don't waste your life
living out other people's expectations.

Don't waste your life
envious of other people.

Be authentic.
Be genuine.
Be real.
Be yourself.

You won the lottery, you were born.
You won the lottery, you are you.

You are Buddha in Blue Jeans.

Enjoy being yourself!

You will learn this sitting quietly.

LIVE EACH MOMENT WELL

Now is all you've got.

The past is memory.

The future is wish.

Now is real.

Keep bringing yourself back to now.

Get connected to your body now.

Get connected to the earth now.

Get connected to this place now.

Get connected to people now.

Get connected to whatever
is in front of you now.

Enjoy living each moment well!

You will learn this sitting quietly.

LOVE INDISCRIMINATELY

Love Indiscriminately.
This is Big Love.

The object of your love
doesn't matter.
You are love.

Love so-called pretty things
and so-called ugly things.

Love familiar things and unfamiliar things.
Love people you like and don't like.

The ocean of love flows everywhere.

Everything in the universe is you.
Loving everything is loving you.
Loving you is loving everything.
There are no walls in the world of love.

Enjoy loving indiscriminately!

You will learn this sitting quietly.

LISTEN TO OTHERS

Listening to others affirms them,
blesses them, connects you to them,
and harmonize you with them.

Listen without an agenda.
Listen without expectations.

Listen to the words.
Listen to the experience
behind the words.

Listen to body postures and expressions.
Listen to emotional tone.

Listen without taking it personally.

Listening gets you out
of your self centered camp.

Listening is kindness.

Enjoy listening to others!

You will learn this sitting quietly.

Be Surprised

Every moment is a surprise.

Everything that happens is a surprise.
Every experience is fresh.

Events are not your ideas about them.
Meet the world without expectations.

Enjoy being surprised!

You will learn this sitting quietly.

WONDER

The world is wonder.

In wonder everything is connected.

In wonder you are open.

In wonder you are free.

In wonder you are happy.

Enjoy wonder!

You will learn this sitting quietly.

LIVE GRATEFULLY

You were given the gift of life.

Be grateful for this amazing gift.

Everything is a gift.

Be grateful for everything.

Enjoy living gratefully.

You will learn this sitting quietly.

Do No Harm

Do your best to do no harm.

Harm happens because we are human.

Forgive others their harm.

Forgive yourself when you harm.

Keep doing your best to do no harm.

You will learn this sitting quietly.

Benefit life

Give yourself to life.

Give yourself to family.

Give yourself to society.

Give yourself to others.

Give yourself to creativity.

Give yourself to the earth.

Give yourself to humanity.

Give yourself to spirituality.

Give yourself to things that matter.

Benefit all life and bring happiness.

Enjoy benefiting life!

You will learn this sitting quietly.

A Wish for The World

May All Beings Be Happy!

May All Beings Be One!

May All Beings Be Peaceful!

You will learn this sitting quietly.

About the Author

Tai Sheridan, Ph.d., is a Poet-philosopher,
with degrees in anthropology and psychology, and a Zen
priest in the Shunryu Suzuki lineage. He trained with San
Francisco Zen Center, Dharma Eye Zen Center,
Berkeley Zen Center, Zen Heart Sangha,
and The Shogaku Zen Institute.

He specializes in transforming
ancient Buddhist and spiritual texts
into accessible and inspirational verses.

Please visit www.taisheridan.com
to review, purchase, or download other
books and podcasts by this author.

You can contact the author at tai@taisheridan.com

Made in the USA
San Bernardino, CA
21 July 2014